IMAGES
of America

FRAMINGHAM

Old Academy Museum

Edgell Memorial Library

Founded in 1888, the Framingham Historical Society is dedicated to fostering an understanding and appreciation of Framingham's rich cultural heritage. The Society operates the Old Academy Museum at Vernon and Grove Streets and offers programs at the Memorial Library on Oak Street.

Our charming cover photograph was taken in June 1912, when several sixth grade students from the Framingham State Normal Practice School, marched to the steps of Edgell Memorial Library. There they recited together a poem beginning, "Hats off! The flag is passing by!" and presented a plaque to be placed in the library.

From left to right are: (front row) Claire Winch, Jeannie Svenson, Lottie Mabie, Helen Reddy, Christine Mullens, Howard Bennett, and Julian Harrington; (back row) Harriet Winch, unidentified, Frances Cushman, Ysabel Hutchinson, Margaret Henderson, and Edith Lindsay. (Photograph by Cokell, from the archives of the Daughters of the American Revolution, gift of Elizabeth van Praag Dudley, FHS Collections.)

IMAGES
of America

FRAMINGHAM

Laurie Evans-Daly & David C. Gordon
Framingham Historical Society

ARCADIA

First published 1997
Copyright © Laurie Evans-Daly and David C. Gordon,
Framingham Historical Society 1997

ISBN 0-7524-0584-5

Published by Arcadia Publishing,
an imprint of the Chalford Publishing Corporation,
One Washington Center, Dover, New Hampshire 03820.
Printed in Great Britain

Library of Congress Cataloging-in-Publication Data applied for

Contents

Acknowledgments   6

Introduction   7

Map   8

1.   Saxonville   9

2.   Framingham Center   23

3.   South Framingham I   43

4.   South Framingham II   63

5.   South Framingham III   81

6.   Nobscot   97

7.   Route 9   111

Acknowledgments

The completion of most large undertakings is generally beyond the scope of one or two people working alone. So it was with this book. Without generous access to the files and collections of the Framingham Historical Society, and the skill and knowledge contributed by staff and members of the Society, this book would not have been possible.

The authors would like to thank several of the Society's members in particular for their contributions.

Ed Convery donated many hours searching the Society's collections and files. In addition, his knowledge added to our understanding of many subjects.

Bonnie Bryant meticulously researched information, and her personal knowledge of Framingham's history contributed to our comprehension when we had gone astray.

For decades Molly Scott Evans has dedicated herself to documenting the history of Framingham through her own photographs and by rephotographing earlier fragile prints. She has generously shared her images with the Society. Many of the photographs included in this book were taken by Molly.

A number of images are from Roger Heinen's personal postcard collection. Roger not only shared his research regarding the postcards but provided information on other topics as well.

Bob Jachowicz contributed to the book's visual appeal by helping with layout and assisting in photo cropping decisions. Bob also drew the map of Framingham which appears on p. 8.

Mention must also be made of the critical contributions made by Ann Welles, Mary Murphy, and Stephen Herring. Ann and Mary cheerfully and encouragingly proofread our text. Stephen Herring, Framingham Town Historian, reviewed our work for historical content. Their skill and knowledge enhanced this book. Revisions to the text were required as the manuscript evolved, and any errors or omissions that may have crept into the final product are solely the responsibility of the authors.

Finally, without the support, encouragement, and direction provided by Carolyn Maguire, Curator/Director of the Framingham Historical Society, this project might never have come to fruition.

Introduction

For thousands of years, Native Americans inhabited the rolling upland area we know as Framingham, Massachusetts. They fished its lakes and streams, hunted game in its forests, and cultivated its fertile soil. Then, 350 years ago, an English colonist named John Stone built a house and mill at the falls on one of these streams, at a place we now call Saxonville. The arrival of this first European settler began the migration of new people into the area.

A slow progression of explorers, land speculators, and settlers followed Stone into this wilderness. As the European population grew, the area became known as Danforth Farms after Thomas Danforth, a leading Bay Colony official, born in Framlingham, England. The settlement incorporated in 1700 as the Town of Framingham.

Eighteenth-century Framingham was an agrarian society, but that changed shortly after 1800. The town's location midway between Boston and Worcester placed Framingham at the center of an evolving transportation network. Improved access to markets beyond the town's borders rapidly shifted Framingham's economy to manufacturing and commerce.

Since 1945 high technology businesses and retail centers located along Route 9 have contributed to Framingham's robust economy and dynamic population growth.

Much information regarding these last 350 years has been recorded in the form of town, county, and state records; personal letters and diaries; newspapers; and various other documents. A number of books and pamphlets based upon the study and interpretation of original documents are available.

With the development of modern photography in the mid-nineteenth century, a new medium was available for the recording of history. This book makes use of photographic images supplemented with occasional drawings, maps, and paintings not only to portray various aspects of the town's history but also to create a visual sense of time and place for this town called Framingham.

Most of the images in this book were gathered from the files and collections of the Framingham Historical Society as noted in the text accompanying each image. Where the identity of the photographer or artist is known, credit is given.

The material in this book has been segmented to coincide with the geographical areas of the town: Saxonville, Framingham Center, South Framingham, Nobscot, and Route 9. Images within each section are generally arranged chronologically. There are, of course, portions of the town's history that are not documented, due to the lack of suitable images.

Finally, we hope that you derive as much enjoyment viewing and reading this book as we did in preparing it.

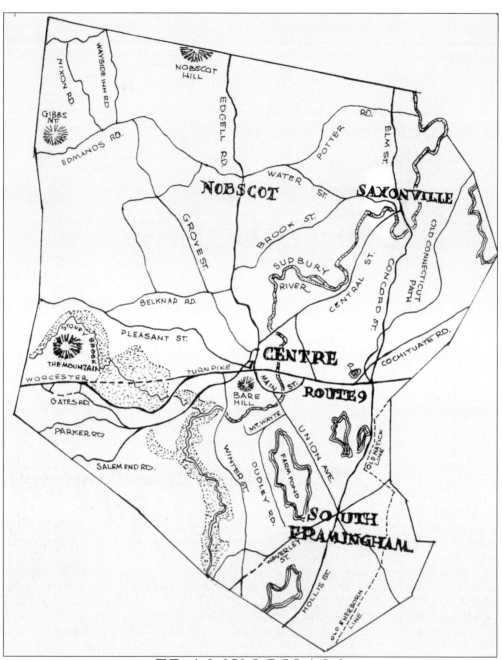

FRAMINGHAM

Map by Bob Jachowicz, 1997
Based upon 1832 Nixon Map
Not drawn to scale

One

Saxonville

Saxonville is named after the Saxon Factory Company, a woolen mill established there in 1824 by Abner, Benjamin, and Eliphalet Wheeler with several Boston partners. Later owners Michael Simpson and Nathaniel Francis changed the factory's name to the Saxonville Mills. Saxonville Mills merged with the Roxbury Carpet Company in 1919 and assumed the name of the latter. (From an 1859 painting of the Saxonville Mills by Dr. Enos Bigelow.)

Michael H. Simpson (1809–84) was proprietor of the Saxonville Mills. A benevolent industrialist, Simpson built parks and donated land and money to public projects for the benefit and enjoyment of all. (M.S. Evans, photographer, FHS Collections.)

Simpson built his mansion, called "the Cottage," prior to 1871, on the west side of Elm Street at the top of the hill, north of today's McGrath Square. Following the death of Simpson's son Frank, the house was sold. Eventually a portion of the mansion was used as a public dance hall known as "The Casino." The house was torn down in 1935. (M.S. Evans, photographer, FHS Collections.)

An interior view of the organ room in Simpson's mansion shows luxurious living at the height of the Victorian era. (M.S. Evans, photographer, courtesy of M.C. Esty, FHS Collections.)

Several boys are shown playing on an early bridge spanning the Sudbury River at the dam, with the original Saxonville Mills complex in the background. The tower held a silver Paul Revere bell which called workers to their tasks each morning. The wooden buildings were destroyed by fire in 1883. The mill was rebuilt in brick and still exists today. (FHS Collections.)

The women shown here are "mule spinning" woolen yarn. At left, wool is being wound from bobbins to springs prior to dyeing. (FHS Collections.)

Weaving Axminster rugs at the Roxbury Carpet Company was serious business. An Axminster rug was a high-pile, quality carpet offered in a wide range of patterns and colors. They were popular in the first half of the twentieth century. (FHS Collections.)

This early 1900s postcard shows Liberty Square, later renamed James J. McGrath Square for a resident who was killed in World War I. Central Street (with trolley tracks) enters from the left, and Elm Street goes right. A town pump is at the base of the tree in the center. The buildings exist today. (Roger Heinen Postcard Collection.)

Traveling southwest on Central Street from Saxonville to Framingham Centre, the building seen in the left foreground is a corner of the Roxbury Carpet mill. The right-side-equipped automobile is turning off Central onto Water Street. (FHS Collections.)

This photograph shows Elm Street at Saxonville going north up "Cottage Hill," so called because Michael Simpson's mansion, "the Cottage," was located just out of view to the left at the crest of the hill along this road. (M.S. Evans, photographer, FHS Collections.)

The Roxbury Carpet Company had become an industrial park by the time this 1975 photograph was taken, looking down Elm Street toward McGrath Square. (*Framingham 275th Anniversary*, courtesy Town of Framingham.)

The railroad station at Saxonville featured an "eyebrow window" in the style of H.H. Richardson. Saxonville station was the end of the line; note an iron barricade at the end of the tracks. The foundation of the roundhouse, used to turn locomotives, was discovered in 1979 near the intersection of Concord and Fuller Streets during excavation for the Saxonville Village apartments. (FHS Collections.)

Boston and Albany railroad engine #205 is seen here leaving Saxonville station in the 1880s. Railroad service to Saxonville began in 1846 and continued until 1936. (M.S. Evans, photographer, FHS Collections.)

This building was built in 1857 and served as Saxonville's high school until the 1890s, when students began taking the trolley to the high school at the Centre. The building continued to house various grammar, junior high, and elementary classrooms until 1923, when it was razed to make way for what is now the Stapleton School. (*Framingham Illustrated*, 1880.)

The Saxonville High School Class of 1888 poses for a photograph. (FHS Collections.)

Town Hall and Engine House, Saxonville, Mass.

J. F. Eber.

Constructed in 1847 at Concord Street and Watson Place, Saxonville's Athenaeum Hall (foreground) was used for meetings, rallies, socials, a temporary hospital, and veterans' functions. It served a dual purpose as a schoolhouse until 1857. The fire station (rear) was built in 1902. A weather vane is mounted atop the station's hose drying tower. Both buildings exist today. (FHS Collections.)

Bowman's Brook flowed through a park built by Michael Simpson. The park presented a fine scene from Simpson's mansion, which had a commanding view from the top of a hill. The brook was later diverted through a culvert and the Pinefield Shopping Center was built on the location. (*Framingham Illustrated*, 1880.)

18

Saxonville and the Sudbury River are shown here in 1876 from Water Street. On the far shore are tenements which mill owner Michael Simpson built for his workers. The structure still exists on Centennial Place. (*Framingham Illustrated*, 1880.)

The beautiful park that Simpson created on the banks of the Sudbury River in Saxonville in the late 1800s was still lovely when this photograph was taken *c.* 1900. (M.S. Evans, photographer, FHS Collections.)

Located just off Potter Road on the Sudbury River at the Framingham/Wayland line, this four-arch stone bridge, dating back to 1860, still stands. The Framingham riverbank, on the left, was washed away by a 1950s hurricane. General Knox's cannon train is said to have crossed an earlier bridge at the same site on the way from Ticonderoga to Boston in 1776. (G.F. Marlowe, photographer, FHS Collections.)

Photographed in 1925, the old gristmill on Cochituate Brook near Old Connecticut Path was torn down c. 1932. (FHS Collections.)

The John Bent House, c. 1665, is Framingham's oldest home. Originally located on Old Connecticut Path, the house was moved to its present site on Concord Street about 1740. (FHS Collections.)

Croquet was frequently played by families during Sunday afternoon gatherings. Michael Simpson (in the tall hat) is enjoying a game with his wife, daughter, and Julia and Joseph Lord c. 1867. (M.S. Evans, photographer, FHS Collections.)

The Sudbury River still cascades over the dam in Saxonville, but "The Falls" referred to in Framingham's earliest records are gone. This area was used by local Native Americans as a fishing ground during salmon migrations. Water power from the river was harnessed as early as 1659 to run John Stone's corn mill. (FHS Collections.)

Two
Framingham Center

This pen and ink drawing by Framingham artist Margaret Kendall (1903–92), after a watercolor by Captain Daniel Bell, shows Bell standing in the foreground sketching. Abner Wheeler is talking to his future wife in the door of his tavern. The house of Rev. Dr. Kellogg, built in 1747, stands in the distance, center right. It is the only building in this picture still standing. As a stagecoach stop on the 40-mile Worcester Turnpike, Framingham Centre grew in size and importance. The area is now a local and national historic district. (Copyright FHS.)

This is Framingham Centre as it appeared in 1875, approaching from the east along Eastern Avenue, now Worcester Road. The buildings, tree, and water trough in the left foreground would make way for the construction of Route 9 in the 1930s. (*Framingham Illustrated*, 1880.)

The Framingham Hotel was built in 1796 and demolished in 1930 after many remodelings and several fires. A landmark round office building, formerly a library, now occupies the site. (*Framingham Illustrated*, 1880.)

Named after Moses Edgell, the town's first free-standing public library was built as a Civil War memorial in 1872. The original building was subsequently enlarged with money donated by Maria Scott Gordon, widow of Civil War General George H. Gordon. Today the building is used by the Framingham Historical Society. (*Framingham Illustrated*, 1880.)

A muddy Edgell Road runs south toward the Centre in this 1876 photograph. Some of the many trees lining the common were felled when the road was widened and paved; others were lost to age and disease. (M.S. Evans, photographer, FHS Collections.)

Neither of the churches in this 1876 view of Framingham Centre stand today. The church on the left was destroyed by fire in 1920, and the other church was razed in 1967. First Parish Unitarian Universalist and Plymouth Church UCC now respectively occupy these sites. (M.S. Evans, photographer, FHS Collections.)

Village Hall was built c. 1834 on the south side of Centre Common to replace a small, wooden town house that was located near the common. A north portico was added in 1907. When town meetings outgrew this facility, various South Framingham locations were utilized until the Memorial Building was erected in 1928. Village Hall is now used for social and civic functions. (*Framingham Illustrated*, 1880.)

The high school at the Centre in 1880 stood to the left of the Old Academy on the common. Later the high school was moved to Pleasant Street at the Centre, where it still exists as an office building. In 1916 the Jonathan Maynard Elementary School was built on the high school site. The Jonathan Maynard building and the Old Academy still exist. (*Framingham Illustrated*, 1880.)

Built in 1837 on the site of an earlier schoolhouse, the Old Academy was originally a private school. Later it became the town's first high school. By the turn of the century, it was used as an elementary school, as shown here. The Framingham Historical Society has leased the building from the town since 1916. (FHS Collections.)

Established in 1839 as the first public teachers' college in the nation, the State Normal School moved to Bare Hill in Framingham in 1853 and eventually became Framingham State College. Saint John's Episcopal Church, designed by Alexander Rice Esty *c.* 1870, was prominent on Bare Hill when this 1876 photograph was taken. It exists today as part of the Framingham State campus. On the left is Normal Hall, also designed by Esty, built in 1853 when the school relocated to Framingham. (M.S. Evans, photographer, FHS Collections.)

When Normal Hall was destroyed by fire in 1889, May Hall was built in its place. Many of May Hall's roof features, shown in this 1896 photograph, were lost in the Hurricane of 1938. The building was repaired and still serves the college today. (FHS Collections.)

Women in 1894 had few career options, but teaching was one of them. These students at the State Normal School in Framingham listen attentively as they prepare for their profession. The first all-campus four-year class graduated in 1939. The undergraduate school remained all female until 1964. (A.H. Folsom, photographer, FHS Collections.)

The Framingham Bank was incorporated in 1833 and operated out of this building. Prior to its incorporation the nearest bank had been in Dedham. The bank relocated to a new building across the street, and a market moved into this one. (FHS Collections.)

The old bank building was moved in December 1968, in preparation for the construction of an underpass at the intersection of Route 9 and Edgell Road. The building is shown raised off its foundation prior to relocation. (M.S. Evans, photographer, FHS Collections.)

The bank building is underway. The white building in the foreground near the northeast corner of Route 9 and Edgell Road was the Increase Sumner Wheeler House. Modern commercial buildings now occupy the space. (M.S. Evans, photographer, FHS Collections.)

The original bank building at its new location on Edgell Road became the center section of what is now the Fleet Bank—preserving an old building for an appropriate reuse. (M.S. Evans, photographer, FHS Collections.)

The gate posts at the historic 28-acre Edgell Grove Cemetery were designed by prominent Framingham architect Alexander Rice Esty in 1878. The 1848 cemetery was influenced by a new movement to create a park-like environment for memorializing the dead. Mount Auburn Cemetery in Cambridge was the first example of this new concept. (*Framingham Illustrated*, 1880.)

The chapel in Edgell Grove Cemetery was designed by Frank Hurd in 1885 and built with a bequest from Moses Edgell. Its lovely painted interior and stained-glass windows were restored in 1988. (FHS Collections.)

The First Baptist Church, with its Christopher Wren spire, is the oldest public building in Framingham. Designed by well-known Boston architect Solomon Willard, the church is listed on both the National Register of Historic Places and on the Historic American Buildings Survey. The wooden structure was built in 1826. Electric lighting was added in 1902. (*Framingham Illustrated*, 1880.)

Fire destroyed many buildings when firefighting equipment was meager and response time was slow. On Easter morning, 1920, a crowd gathered to grieve the loss of First Parish's meetinghouse at the Centre Common. A new brick meetinghouse was built on the site several years later. (M.S. Evans, photographer, FHS Collections.)

Suffering from ill health, Wallace Nutting (1861–1941) left the ministry at age forty-three and pursued his avocation of photographing landscapes and colonial interiors. He produced over 10,000 different titles and sold millions of hand-colored platinum prints. Nutting did more than any figure of his time to popularize interest in artifacts from America's colonial past. (Courtesy Louis M. MacKeil, FHS Collections.)

Wallace Nutting moved his Early American furniture reproduction business to 46 Park Street in 1926. Chair #420, shown here, sold for $40 at the time. (*Wallace Nutting Period Sales* brochure, FHS Collections.)

THE WALLACE NUTTING HOME. FRAMINGHAM. MASS.

Wallace Nutting and his wife, Mariet Griswold Caswell, purchased their home on Vernon Street, Framingham Centre, in 1912 and lived out their lives there. The building was torn down in 1961. (FHS Collections.)

This *c.* 1900 view shows a bowstring pony-truss bridge over the Sudbury River at Summer Street, now Central Street. The bridge was named for Civil War General George H. Gordon, who lived nearby. A concrete bridge erected in 1969 now spans the river at this site. (FHS Collections.)

The boathouse of the Framingham Canoe Club was on the east bank of the Sudbury River, across from today's Sudbury River Tennis Club on Edgell Road. One could paddle upstream to the dam at Winter Street and downstream to the dam at Fenwick Street. (FHS Collections.)

A graduate of West Point, George H. Gordon of Framingham was severely wounded in the Mexican-American War. At the outbreak of the Civil War Gordon raised and commanded the Second Massachusetts Regiment of Infantry. A gallant soldier, he was promoted to brigadier general during the war. General Gordon returned to Framingham following the war, where he practiced law and wrote several books. (Carte de Visite, Brady's Nat'l Portrait Gallery, FHS Collections.)

This view of Gordon's Corner, looking north in the early 1900s, shows Edgell Road continuing along on the left and Central Street coming in on the right. Both were dirt roads at the time. The signpost and large oak exist today. (FHS Collections.)

Inaugural Race Meeting

AT

"RACELAND"

ESTATE OF

Mr. JOHN R. MACOMBER

FRAMINGHAM CENTRE. MASS.

Saturday, June 18, 1927

First Race Called at 2.30 o'clock

UNDER THE MANAGEMENT OF THE

EASTERN HORSE CLUB

Sanctioned by the Hunts Committee of the
National Steeplechase and Hunt Association

STEWARDS OF MEETING

AUGUSTUS F. GOODWIN	BAYARD TUCKERMAN, JR.
JOHN R. MACOMBER	HENRY G. VAUGHAN
F. S. von STADE	BAYARD WARREN

BOARD OF STEWARDS

AUGUSTUS F. GOODWIN, Chairman

CHARLES F. ADAMS	A. HENRY HIGGINSON
WILLIAM ALMY, JR.	WILLIAM W. HOLBROOK
JAMES W. APPLETON	JOHN F. JORDAN
REGINALD W. BIRD	JOHN R. MACOMBER
CHARLES S. BIRD, JR.	ADNAH NEYHART
EDWARD W. BLODGETT	HARRY C. RICE
JOHN P. BOWDITCH	HARRY W. SMITH
EDGAR A. BOWERS	PIERPONT L. STACKPOLE
BENJAMIN L. COOK	BAYARD TUCKERMAN, JR.
RICHARD E. DANIELSON	HENRY G. VAUGHAN
B. NASON HAMLIN	BAYARD WARREN

Frank J. Bryan

Racing Secretary

PRICE 15 CENTS

John Macomber built a private racetrack at his "Raceland" estate on Salem End Road for flat and steeplechase racing of thoroughbreds. Races held there attracted up to 25,000 visitors. The race card pictured was for the inaugural meet. The mansion at Raceland was built in 1925 with attached stables; Macomber occasionally brought horses into the living room in order to show them to his surprised guests. The original wooden mansion burned in 1930, was rebuilt in cement and brick, and stands today as a private residence. (FHS Collections.)

The stables at Raceland were built of mahogany. The horses lived in surroundings almost as elegant as their master's. (House of Photography, Inc., FHS Collections.)

The Pike-Haven House, c. 1697, on the corner of Grove Street and Belknap Road, is one of Framingham's oldest homes still standing on its original site. The Pike family manufactured spinning wheels for several generations. (M.S. Evans, photographer, FHS Collections.)

The "Old Burying Ground" on Main Street off Buckminster Square was the site of the first meetinghouse. At the time of the town's incorporation in 1700, the meetinghouse served as a place for both religious services and town meetings. A new meetinghouse was constructed on the Centre Common in 1735. (M.S. Evans, photographer, FHS Collections.)

THIS TABLET MARKS
THE SPOT ON WHICH STOOD
THE DWELLING HOUSE OF
THE REV D
JOHN SWIFT
FIRST MINISTER
OF FRAMINGHAM
BORN IN MILTON MASS MAR 14
1678 9 GRADUATED FROM
HARVARD COLLEGE 1697
ORDAINED AT FRAMINGHAM
OCT 8 1701 DIED APRIL 24
1745 IN THE FORTY FOURTH
YEAR OF HIS MINISTRY IN
FRAMINGHAM
JAM TANDEM IN DOMINO
REQUIE VIT
PLACED BY THE FRAMINGHAM HISTORICAL AND NATURAL
HISTORY SOCIETY JUNE 17 1911

The Reverend John Swift, Framingham's first settled minister, served from 1701 to 1745. The site of his house on Maple Street is commemorated with a granite marker. Reverend Swift is buried in the "Old Burying Ground," at the site where his pulpit stood. (M.S. Evans, photographer, FHS Collections.)

The Minute Man Monument at Buckminster Square was dedicated in June 1905. Sculptor Henry Hudson Kitson became ill during the work, and his wife, Theo Alice Ruggles Kitson, finished it. This photo shows the statue in its original position at the edge of the square facing southwest. To accommodate automobile traffic, a town meeting voted to relocate the monument to its present location. The Minute Man Monument now faces northeast so that the majority of traffic can view the statue's profile. (FHS Collections.)

Three
South Framingham I

Common and Baptist Church, SOUTH FRAMINGHAM, Mass.

The "Old Field" or "Indian burial ground" is now known as the Downtown or South Common. At the rear is the Park Street Baptist Church, designed by Alexander Rice Esty and erected in 1854. In 1800 South Framingham had only four businesses—a tavern, a store, a cider mill, and a shoe shop. Seven families made up the entire population of the village. (FHS Collections.)

THIS THE "OLD FIELD" OF 1800
WAS AN INDIAN BURIAL GROUND
A TOWN COMMON SINCE 1854
THE GIFT OF LOVELL EAMES

THIS STONE ERECTED UNDER THE
WILL OF WILLIAM HARVEY SMITH
1946

BRONZES REPRESENT LOCAL
INDIAN LIFE THE CENTER
CARRYING OF CORN TO THE
HUNGRY BAY COLONISTS IN 1630
THE NEARBY TRAIL EARLY

The monument above, with its bronze plaques, was erected in 1946 through the kindness of William Harvey Smith to honor Native Americans who, in 1630, walked over 100 miles on what would become Old Connecticut Path to bring corn to starving settlers in Boston. Both this monument and the Old Field commemorative boulder shown at left are located on the South Common along Concord Street. (M.S. Evans, photographer, FHS Collections.)

SITE OF EAMES MASSACRE, MONTWAITE, MASS.

At the outbreak of King Philip's War in 1676, Thomas Eames and his family were living at a place that would later become part of Framingham. While Eames was away in Boston, his homestead was attacked by a band of Native Americans whose cache of food had been pilfered by colonists. His wife and five of their children were slain. Four children were taken captive. This marker stands on the Mt. Wayte site. (FHS Collection.)

In 1721 Henry Eames, grandson of Thomas, built the middle section of the landmark Eames Red House on Union Avenue. A valiant effort in 1969 to keep the building on its site failed. The house was moved to Prospect Street where it stands today. Several apartment buildings were constructed on the original site. (FHS Collections.)

This 1914 postcard shows tin peddler Francis Chickering of Ashland with his horse and wagon selling wares near present-day Dennison Crossing. (FHS Collections.)

The South Framingham Hotel, originally built as a house in 1766, served stagecoach traffic before construction of the railroad. The hotel was closed by its proprietor in 1891 when the town rigidly enforced a law prohibiting liquor sales. The building was razed in 1894. (*Framingham Illustrated*, 1880.)

ICE.

...father having given me entire charge of his
... business, I desire to inform the people of So.
...ramingham that from this date I am prepared
...deliver ice for family use at

20 Cents per 100 Pounds.

Orders by mail promptly attended to, and any
person ordering by mail will receive 25 cents re-
duction on the first month's bill.
By a careful service and the best ice obtain-
able I hope to please the public.

John Willis, Jr.

South Framingham, May 2, 1891.   5-3 dw 1 mo.

A spectacular fire in April 1932 destroyed the Cove Ice storage facility at Waushakum Pond. The blaze illuminated the night sky with such brilliance that folks came from neighboring towns to view the conflagration. Sawdust used as insulation in the walls of the building contributed to the inferno. (Gift of Mrs. William J. Bell, FHS Collections.)

In 1834 plans called for the railroad to pass through Framingham Centre, but several men with special interests in the turnpike and stagecoach line were opposed to that route. Thus the rails were laid two miles further south in South Framingham. The wooden railroad station above was built in 1848 replacing an earlier station. (*Framingham Illustrated*, 1880.)

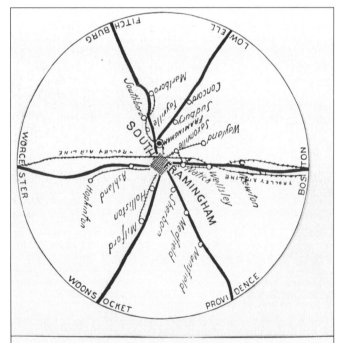

SOUTH FRAMINGHAM

**If not the Hub of the Universe the Hub of a Territory containing
2,000,000 people within a radius of thirty miles**

Trade brochures at the turn of the century used this map to extol South Framingham's rail hub. Six lines converged to make Framingham the center of a regional rail network. The railroad transformed the social and economic life of South Framingham and eventually put the stagecoaches and turnpike out of business. (FHS Collections.)

Bustling activity surrounds the railroad depot in this 1885 view. One hundred trains a day stopped at South Framingham in 1885. In the background is the spire of the Park Street Baptist Church and the four-story Barber straw hat factory which became Wallace Nutting's furniture factory. Both buildings are in use today. (E.O. Waite, photographer, courtesy Society for the Preservation of New England Antiquities.)

Beautiful bull's-eye glass sparkles in the bay window of the ticket master's office in the railroad station designed by H.H. Richardson. Built in 1885, and restored in 1985 by Lew Horton, the station is a restaurant today. It is listed in the National Register of Historic Places and the Historic American Buildings Survey. (M.S. Evans, photographer, FHS Collections.)

In 1885 the new station designed by Richardson was built next to the old wooden one. The old station, here up on timbers, was moved several feet to the west and used as a freight depot. It was eventually torn down. (Courtesy Framingham Public Library.)

A trolley is shown here waiting at the Boston & Albany Railroad station in Framingham in 1912. The granite-block station simultaneously served the rail and trolley lines. (M.S. Evans, photographer, FHS Collections.)

On the back of this photograph is the following inscription, "February 2, 1898, Framingham snowplow train met at Marlboro Junction, a milk train and helped by the plow, landed on top!" (Wade, photographer, FHS Collections.)

The last Boston & Albany steam train passes through Framingham on April 16, 1951.

The last Boston & Albany steam train passed through Framingham on April 16, 1951. Rail travel has experienced a resurgence in recent years, with over 1,000 passengers a day now riding MBTA commuter trains to Boston. (FHS Collections.)

1850–1875
HARMONY GROVE
Anti-Slavery Rostrum

GATHERINGS HERE LED THE AGITATION
WHICH RESULTED IN THE ABOLITION OF
SLAVERY IN AMERICA.

FRAMINGHAM HISTORICAL SOCIETY, 1915

In the 1850s Harmony Grove was a popular commercial recreational park located between Farm Pond and Union Avenue. A railroad spur line ran directly into the grounds. The 3/4-acre natural depression that was the amphitheater is most visible from Beech Street. This small marker stands on the southwest corner of Henry and Franklin Streets. (FHS Collections.)

Harmony Grove had ". . . one of the most beautiful and perfect natural amphitheaters . . ." in the country and could seat a thousand people with standing room for more. At one famous gathering in 1854, William Lloyd Garrison burned a copy of the U.S. Constitution in protest of slavery. (Etching from *Gleason's Pictorial Home Companion*, 1852, FHS Collections.)

Framingham Hospital began with a few beds to provide for emergencies, in a house on Winthrop Street in 1893. Most medical care and surgery still took place at home or in a doctor's office. As medical services began to be performed in the hospital, more space was required and Framingham Hospital moved to these buildings on Evergreen Street near Learned Pond. (FHS Collections.)

In 1912 a group of doctors left Framingham Hospital to form Union Avenue Hospital in these two buildings on Union Avenue. The buildings were connected by a passageway. Union Avenue Hospital then merged with Framingham Hospital in 1928. The name became Framingham Union Hospital, located on Evergreen Street. Today the privately owned hospital is called the Columbia Metro West Medical Center. The former hospital buildings on Union Avenue, with passageway, still exist. (FHS Collections.)

The nurses' home for Framingham Hospital was located on Beech Street between Lincoln Street and Learned Pond. Called Day Memorial Hall in honor of its benefactors, the Day brothers, it served Framingham's nurses for some sixty years. (FHS Collections.)

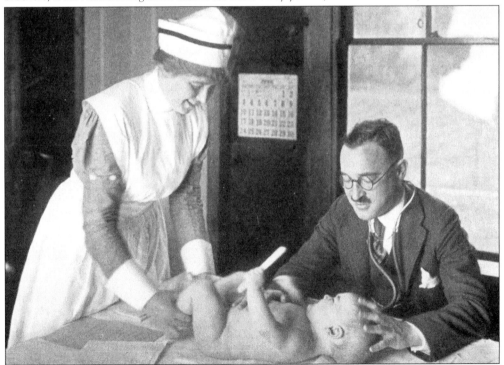

A nurse and doctor are seen here looking over a new citizen. In 1918 a packet of pictures was assembled by the COMFORTS COMMITTEE to cheer up Framingham soldiers fighting in World War I. (FHS Collections.)

The New England Branch of Chautauqua, a center for education, religion, and the arts, was founded at Mt. Wayte in 1874 by two Methodist ministers, Reverends Clark and Winslow. Ten-day sessions featuring lecturers, teachers, and entertainers were held throughout the summer. (J.A. French, photographer, FHS Collections.)

This view of the audience from the stage of the outdoor auditorium shows seating in a grove, with family tents beyond. Small, privately owned, Victorian cottages, many of which still exist, soon replaced tents as the popularity of Chautauqua grew. Thirty-room dormitories and a dining room with seating capacity for three hundred were also available. (J.A. French, photographer, FHS Collections.)

CHAUTAUQUA BELLS AND PART OF PUBLIC BUILDINGS, MONTWAITE, MASS.

The Chautauqua bells rang each morning at 6:30 to awaken participants so that they might greet the sun as it rose over beautiful Farm Pond. The bells called all to meals, celebrated festive occasions, and signaled good night at 10:00 pm. They were last rung on Armistice Day, 1918. (J.A. French, photographer, FHS Collections.)

The New England Branch of Chautauqua at Framingham, also known as Lake View, featured cultural, educational, and recreational opportunities in addition to religious studies. Participants could enroll in a four-year program. Thirty trains a day provided transportation from all over New England. (J.A. French, photographer, FHS Collections.)

Police Department

FRAMINGHAM , MASS.

....19.......

MR ....

Your   REAR - WINDOW   **Was Found Open**
FRONT - DOOR

BY OFFICER ....

Another Safety Item By
American Safety League

TIME .... **A. M.** .... **P. M.**
Edward T. McCarthy, Chief of Police

In the 1940s Framingham police, by leaving a card like this, were gracious enough to inform citizens that they had left a window open or a door unlocked at a business, home, or automobile. At night, police would close the window or bar the door, allowing owners to sleep in peace. (FHS Collections.)

Every parade, in every town, was led by the "Keepers of Order." In 1905 the guardians of the law led the parade to the unveiling of the Minute Man Monument at Buckminster Square. Mounted and on foot, the police are seen here turning off Concord Street heading north onto Union Avenue. (Gift of Dr. Joseph C. Merriam, FHS Collections.)

"Prince" was always ready to help fight Framingham's fires. When an alarm rang, the stall door sprang open and the horse was led to the front of the fire wagon. A suspended harness dropped down and was quickly hitched. The Hollis Street fire station with its hose drying tower still stands. (FHS Collections.)

Engine #3 is parked here in front of the Hollis Street fire station. From 1818 until 1922 Framingham had volunteer fire protection. The first motorized apparatus was purchased in 1918. During World War II an auxiliary fire department was established at the Musterfield. Now five stations and round-the-clock fire personnel are always at the ready. (Phipps, photographer, FHS Collections.)

In this photograph, a crowd gathers to watch the Fourth of July parade in 1890. Some have come on high-wheel bikes, others have the new, easier to ride, safety bikes. Horse-drawn floats head north on Concord Street after leaving Waverley Street. The South Framingham Hotel

was taken down in 1894. The early 1950s "modern" Gilchrist Building, now occupied by the Salvation Army, stands on part of the site where the hotel stood. (Gift of J.J. Valkenburg, FHS Collections.)

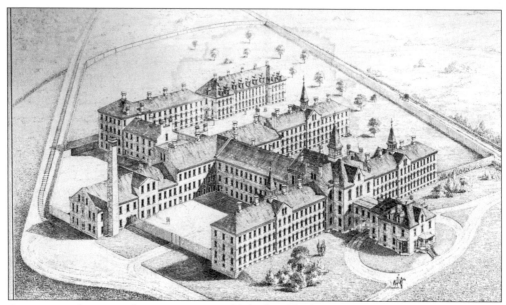

A separate reformatory for women was established in Sherborn in 1877 to prevent the abuse of women that occurred when housed in the general prison system. In 1924 a change in town boundaries put the prison in Framingham. Today it is known as MCI-Framingham; it remains a facility for women. Several older structures, including the original superintendent's building, still exist. (Engraving by Geo. Ropes, engraver, FHS Collections.)

Clara Barton, founder of the American Red Cross, was an early superintendent at the prison. She accepted the position as a favor to Governor Benjamin Bulter who, as a general, had been her colleague and advocate during the Civil War. (FHS Collections.)

Four

South Framingham II

Two different kinds of trolleys can be seen south of the common, a Boston-South Framingham car on the right and a Hudson-bound open bench car on the left. Also visible in this c. 1900 South Framingham street view is the front of the Nobscot Block, which stood at the southwest corner of Concord and Howard Streets. The trees in the background on the far right are where today's Memorial Building stands. (Roger Heinen Postcard Collection.)

Set up on the South Common in 1917, this farmyard scene was supposed to teach people the correct way to handle milk. By today's standards of pasteurization and sanitation, even the "clean way" of handling milk would hardly be considered "correct." (FHS Collections.)

George H. and Arthur M. Fitts built a store on the corner of Union Avenue and Concord Street sometime after 1883. They became a large household supply store with branches in five towns. Arthur M. was well known and a leading citizen in town. (M.S. Evans, photographer, FHS Collections.)

The handsome Waverley Building stood at the corner of Waverley Street and Irving Square. It was South Framingham's first commercial block building. It burned down in 1905 and was replaced by the brick Bullard Building, which now holds a dental clinic. (*Framingham Illustrated*, 1880.)

Grandpa William Woodward sits in his milk wagon while his driver, Ned Doran, manages the horse. The photograph was taken around 1900. (U.S. Photograph Co., FHS Collections.)

In 1871 the Nobscot Building, located on the corner of Concord and Howard Streets, was constructed for the manufacture of wheels. Clifford Folger's department store occupied part of the building at the time of this photograph. The structure was razed in 1939. (*Framingham Illustrated*, 1880.)

The Eagles held this picnic sometime before World War I. Florist J. Seaver, whose business still exists, is third from the left. From the right, William McDonald is third; Ed Kernan, fourth; and Mr. Healy, sixth. (FHS Collections.)

A huge arch was erected in honor of those who served in the Spanish-American War of 1898. Note the horse-drawn trolley. (FHS Collections.)

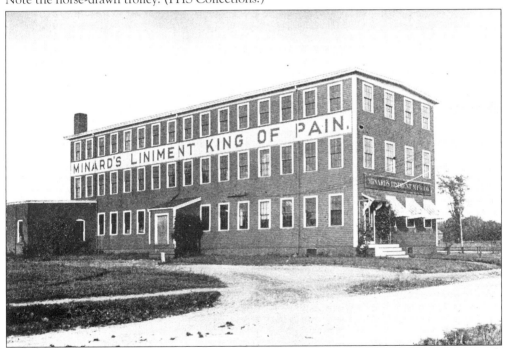

In 1904 the owners of Minard's Liniment were so pleased with everything they saw in South Framingham that they moved their business from Boston to a vacant harness factory on Summit Street. Besides their famous liniment, they also manufactured athlete's rub, milk of magnesia, nose & throat drops, wave set, and imitation vanilla. (M.S. Evans, photographer, FHS Collections.)

The A.H. Ordway Company manufactured wicker chairs. Ordway originated and patented a base rocker design. He also pioneered selling chairs "from a team" (horse and wagon) and buying "on time." His factory, pictured here in 1889, was located on Wellington Avenue near the Sherborn line. It burned in 1902. (FHS Collections.)

Coburnville, c. 1875, was a section of South Framingham near Waverley and Bridges Streets. An 1883 *Framingham Gazette* advertisement says that the area was destined to become a very pleasant locality for residences. Ten double-tenement houses had just been completed, and fifty additional were needed for boot shop employees. (Drake Photograph Studio, FHS Collections.)

Shipping tags, mostly made from left-over cardboard, were known as "direction labels" before the Civil War. The possibilities were seen by E.W. Dennison and in 1893 he patented a tag reinforced with paper washers. Shipping tags became one of the Dennison Manufacturing Company's largest and most visible product lines, giving Framingham the nickname "Tag Town." This early photograph shows the Dennison plant in downtown Framingham. (FHS Collections.)

Founded in 1844 in Brunswick, Maine, the Dennison Manufacturing Company consolidated its many-cited operation in 1897 by moving into existing factory buildings in Framingham. This early view, looking north across Howard and Bishop Streets, shows the Dennison sign on the building. Today the complex is owned by the South Middlesex Opportunity Council. (Roger Heinen Postcard Collection.)

Dennison was ahead of its time in arranging transportation to the job for its workers. Some of these factory hands may have come from row houses that still exist on Grant Street. (FHS Collections.)

In Department 28, rolls of tag stock were split into smaller rolls, the width of which represented the length of a tag. (FHS Collections.)

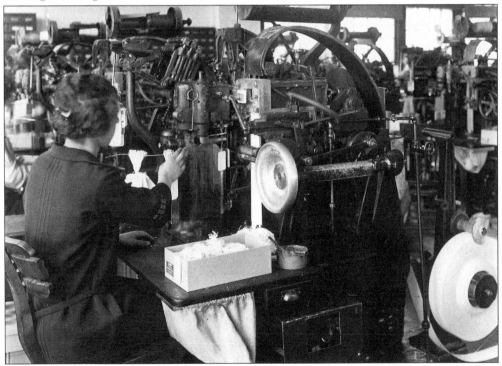

Before machines like this, stringing tags was a cottage industry. All over Framingham women and children augmented their income by threading and tying strings in tags in their homes for the Dennison Manufacturing Company. (FHS Collections.)

A crepe printer in the crepe paper department at Dennison is printing flag designs in this *c.* 1900 photograph. (FHS Collections.)

Dennison was known as a people-oriented company where a shipping clerk could work his way to the top like a character in an Horatio Alger novel. (FHS Collections.)

Seen from the north along Irving Street, the First Methodist Episcopal Church of South Framingham is the first building on the left. Next is the Tribune Building where Framingham's first daily newspaper, *The Tribune*, began publication in 1890. At right is the Twombly Building which was destroyed by fire in 1933. The church was razed in 1917, but the Tribune Building still stands. (Roger Heinen Postcard Collection.)

The name Waushakum was contracted from the Algonquin word "washakamaug," meaning "eel-fishing place." Waushakum actually referred to a connecting waterway that once existed between Lake Waushakum, shown here, and Farm Pond. Native Americans would gather to catch eels along this waterway. The Nipmucs, in particular, prized eels. (FHS Collections.)

George Hooker is seen here using a small hand-held scale to weigh a chicken near his meat wagon in the early 1900s. Hopefully he had some ice aboard to keep his meats cold. The horse waits patiently for his master to complete the sale. (Gift of Hazel M. Davis, FHS Collections.)

Dan Cooney won a bet with Dr. Palmer over the 1892 presidential race between Cleveland and Harrison. Mr. Cooney furnished the wagon and four-horse team and then risked his life as a passenger while Dr. Palmer experimented with the reins. The picture was taken in Irving Square; the First Methodist Episcopal Church is on the extreme right. (FHS Collections.)

74

C.S. Oaks ran a grocery store that was typical of its time with sawdust on the floor, cracker barrels, and strategically located spittoons. (M.S. Evans, photographer, FHS Collections.)

The elm that stood on Concord Street next to the South Framingham Hotel (see the bottom of p. 46) had been planted in 1773 by Moses Eames. The tree was taken down in 1888. The event attracted plenty of interest among the men in town. Note the proud owner of a high-wheel bike leaning his vehicle against the tree trunk. (FHS Collections.)

The Framingham Gazette, established as a weekly newspaper in 1871 by the firm of Pratt and Wood, lasted for fifty years. This photograph shows the Union Block on Waverley Street, home of *The Gazette*, in 1880. The third floor was later removed. The building survives today across from the railroad station. (*Framingham Illustrated*, 1880.)

With "stovepipe" hats, Chesterfield coats, and silver-headed canes, Pan American Congressional delegates gathered in October 1889 at the Para Rubber Company, at the corner of Howard and Bishop Streets (the Dennison Manufacturing Company later occupied the buildings). The group toured the facilities and observed rubber boot and shoe manufacturing. Lining the street in welcome were five hundred schoolchildren, while American, Spanish, and Portuguese flags flew proudly. (FHS Collections.)

Built in 1876, Odd Fellows Hall on Hollis Street is downtown Framingham's oldest standing masonry commercial building. Unfortunately, the wonderful mansard roof was removed in 1928 to "modernize" the building; however, the sides and back remain unchanged. (*Framingham Illustrated*, 1880.)

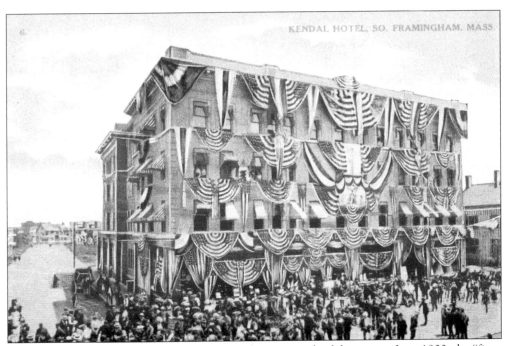

Decked out in flags and bunting for the town's bicentennial celebration in June 1900, the "first-class" Kendall Hotel had been open only a year. Located on Concord Street at the corner of Kendall Street, the hotel offered steam heat, in-suite baths, an elevator, a barbershop, billiards, and bowling. The building stands today. (FHS Collections.)

HOTEL WINTHROP

HOLLIS ST., SOUTH FRAMINGHAM, MASS.

The Winthrop Hotel was built *c.* 1882 by Simon O'Connell of Hopkinton. Located on Hollis Street, the hotel was a two-minute walk from the depot. (FHS Collections.)

This *c.* 1912 photograph of the Winthrop Hotel shows its full three-story front after enlargement. The building today houses the Turning Point Shelter. (FHS Collections.)

A major disaster occurred on July 23, 1906. The Amsden Building, on the east side of Concord Street, was well along in its construction when it collapsed, killing thirteen workers and injuring more than thirty. The building ultimately was completed and exists today. (FHS Collections.)

The Civic League was constructed in 1916 and stands today on Concord Street near Lincoln Street. An indoor pool was added in 1918 but only operated until 1921. The pool was filled with sand and covered with a gym floor. (Cokell, photographer, FHS Collections.)

The 1897 brick Classical Revival Concord Block, with its interesting arched windows, is still an integral part of South Framingham's streetscape. By the time this photograph was taken in 1910, Clifford Folger's department store had left its previous location at the corner of Concord and Howard Streets and moved into the Concord Block. (FHS Collections.)

The Memorial Building, Framingham's new town hall, was built in 1928 to replace the outgrown Village Hall at the Centre Common. It was named to memorialize "... citizens who served in the nation's wars." The large auditorium, used for town meetings, was named after David Nevins who bequeathed $100,000 toward the construction of a new town hall. (FHS Collections.)

Five
South Framingham III

CONCORD STREET, FRAMINGHAM, MASSACHUSETTS   1697

Concord Street in 1940 looked much as it does today. From left to right are the South Common, the Framingham National Bank (*c.* 1933), the Concord Block (*c.* 1897), the Memorial Building (*c.* 1927), the Amsden Building (*c.* 1908), the Kendall Hotel (*c.* 1899), the St. George Theater (*c.* 1921), and the Park Building (*c.* 1921). All but the last two remain, comprising much of today's Concord Square Historic District. (Roger Heinen Postcard Collection.)

Doing their part on the home front in the summer of 1917, all Framingham schools had a "war garden" as the nation united to fight a war on foreign soil. This picture is from a packet assembled by the COMFORTS COMMITTEE to cheer up our soldiers. (FHS Collections.)

Framingham schools established a six-three-three (elementary-junior high-senior high) system after construction of the Lincoln (c. 1920), Memorial (c. 1920), and Saxonville (c. 1923) junior high schools. Later Lincoln, shown here, served as an elementary school. The building is still owned by the town, but has been privately renovated as part of a fifty-year lease and houses a medical center. (FHS Collections.)

Framingham High School on Union Avenue was erected in 1907, replacing a wooden building at the Centre. It was enlarged twice. In 1958, it became Framingham Junior High; in 1964, Lincoln Junior High; and in 1970, Farley Middle School. The Danforth Museum of Art, the Framingham Park and Recreation Department, and the Callahan Senior Center currently share the building. (Cokell, photographer, FHS Collections.)

The faculty members of Framingham High School are shown here in 1932. From left to right are: (front row) Ross, Hobbs, Richardson, Lawson, Principal Magoon, Bush, Hemenway, and Lundberg; (second row) Stiles, Wiley, Forbes, Whittier, Burnhan, Cunningham, Hall, and McNamara; (third row) Sweeney, Williams, Fairbanks, Ballou, Hill, Squires, and Rogers; (fourth row) Hollander, Barham, Burke, Sweeney, Mason, Leland, Daniels, and Brooks; (back row) Small, Peterson, and Jordan. (Cokell, photographer, FHS Collections.)

Framingham High School's championship girls' basketball team of 1911 posed for this picture. From left to right are Gertrude Barto, Dorothy Avery, captain Pauline Frederick, Gladys Gould, Helena O'Brien, and Nellie Lynch. Their silver cup was placed on display in the school library. (Cokell, photographer, FHS Collections.)

Framingham High School's baseball team of 1907 is shown here, probably before a game or practice (note the lack of dirt or grass on their uniforms). From left to right are: (front row) Paul Neal, Charles Stowers, and Bill Ralston; (middle row) Harold Harney, Tom Hoey, Carl Nichols, and Roland Hueston; (back row) William McCormack, Richard Long, coach Donald McCormack, Harold Brackett, and Michael Dunn. (Cokell, photographer, FHS Collections.)

Harvard's Hasty Pudding had nothing on our Civic League Players of the 1930s. From left to right are A.S. Whiting, J. Whiting, Charles Newcomb, Moses Ellis, and John Macomber. They displayed a variety of emotions in plays like *The Three Cornered Moon*, a whimsical comedy about a slightly zany family. These gentlemen must have been considered audacious for their time. (Gift of M.S. Evans, FHS Collections.)

In the days before washing machines and dryers, linens and other things were frequently sent "to the laundry." Established by L. Russell on Howard Street, the Framingham Laundry was the first steam laundry in Framingham and employed over thirty people. (FHS Collections.)

The newspaper announced "Moths Have Chosen Town For Winter Quarters . . ." when countless thousands of gypsy moths or browntails descended on the town mid-evening on October 19, 1914. The Public Works Department prepared their equipment to combat this horde; after the killing, dead bugs filled downtown gutters. (FHS Collections.)

The COMFORTS COMMITTEE of Framingham Military and Naval Associates was ready to welcome military personnel from the Musterfield. They wanted our "fighting boys" to know their "home folk" were kind and caring. Coffee and famous Framingham doughnuts were offered by vivacious Bloomer Girls from Seaman & Cobb Company. (FHS Collections.)

Aproned for cleanliness, telephone operators work here at a candy pull for Framingham's soldiers and sailors in 1918. The COMFORTS COMMITTEE packets given the soldiers stated "If here, or 'Over There', — 'tis true; These gifts are yours, — for we're no miser; And if they 'Make a Hit' with You; Just do your best to hit the Kaiser!" (FHS Collections.)

Ground was broken on June 2, 1943, for a military hospital named in honor of Dr. Harvey Cushing of World War I fame. Containing 1,750 beds, Cushing General Hospital was located between Winter Street and Dudley Road. Special trains brought soldiers wounded in World War II directly here from hospital ships. Following the Battle of the Bulge, 3,200 soldiers were treated at Cushing. The hospital was also used as a work site for German prisoners of war. (FHS Collections.)

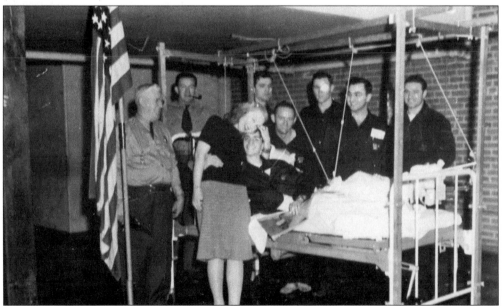

USO entertainers did much to cheer up our wounded soldiers at Cushing General Hospital in the mid-1940s. A woman's touch brought a smile to many who had suffered much. Bob Hope, Benny Goodman, Charlie Spivak, Edgar Bergen & Charlie McCarthy, and heavyweight champion Jack Dempsey were a few big-timers who entertained our service men and women at Cushing. (FHS Collections.)

the
CHART
Cushing General Hospital

VOLUME 2   NUMBER 9   FRAMINGHAM,   MASSACHUSETTS   OCTOBER 1945

IT'S GOODBYE FOREVER

With "ruptured duck" (discharge insignia) on his chest, a smile on his face, and signing-out pay in his pocket, a clean cut, recuperated GI gives a final salute to those at Cushing General Hospital who put him back on his feet. (*The Chart*, Vol. 2, No. 9, October 1945.)

WKOX, Framingham's own radio station, signed on in April 1947. It was limited in its early days to just daytime broadcasting. WKOX was the only station allowed to broadcast from the official Boston Marathon time car until 1982. (Courtesy of Sandy Shurick.)

Famed African-American sculptress Meta Warrick Fuller (1877–1968) was honored by the Framingham Women's Club with a dinner and a corsage. Ms. Fuller studied under Rodin and was a close friend of William E.B. DuBois. She lived with her husband, Dr. Solomon C. Fuller, the first African-American psychiatrist in America, on Warren Road. The Fuller Middle School honors them. (FHS Collections.)

Meta Warrick Fuller's *Emancipation Proclamation*, 1913, celebrating Lincoln's manifesto, depicts humanity pushing forth a young black man and woman to freedom. Fuller provided a "study" for the Jamestown tercentennial in 1907. This "gentle lady with a strong talent" who refused to bow to gender or racial stereotypes was honored at the White House by Theodore Roosevelt. (Courtesy Museum of the Center for Afro-American Artists.)

In 1925 the musical fame of the nine-piece Fred Adams Empire Singing Orchestra, a local group, was ". . . wide and supreme," and they ". . . had to be experienced." The musicians are Frank Slater (drums), Henry Werner (trumpet), Ernest MacGrath (tuba), Joseph Nutter (trombone), Gladys Adams (piano), Fred Woods (saxophone), William Russell (banjo), Fred Adams (saxophone and trumpet), and Launcy Heuston (violin). (FHS Collections.)

The Framingham Rotary Club's forty-seven member band poses c. 1940 in front of Nevins Hall. Dressed in the brilliant uniform of the Algerian French Infantry, their fame preceded their stirring march renditions. (FHS Collections.)

For just a dime, one could enjoy Fritz's Troupe of Trained Dogs or watch "Bob Alexander, the Scientific Nutte," vaudeville, Keystone Comedy, or thrilling shows of the Broncho Company at the Princess Theater. One of the first theaters built for movies in the Boston area, this Concord Street entertainment center served the town from 1908 to 1917. (Roger Heinen Postcard Collection.)

The St. George Theater replaced the Princess Theater in 1921. The St. George was a favorite movie house where many Framingham children watched double features on Saturday afternoons. It was demolished in 1968, and the site became a parking lot. (Shelden A. Glew, photographer, FHS Collections.)

The Drury Building rises over Irving Square, *c.* 1900, and streetcar tracks run down the cobblestone street, harkening to a slower, sweeter life. A water-filled trough for horses, awning-covered windows, bunting, and flags suggest a warm July day. In just a few years all of this would change. (FHS Collection.)

Alas, in 1958, the Drury Building was gone. In its place, a plethora of signs beckoned for purchases of gasoline, beer, fruit, hardware, curtains, and furniture. Today, Burkis Park has replaced Fruitland, and the signs are more subtle. However, Irving Square remains a busy intersection for travel and commerce. (Sheldon A. Glew, photographer, FHS Collections.)

Just over the tracks at Waverley and Concord Streets in 1958, well-stocked shops awaited Monday morning's customers. The tree-shaded common (the old Indian burial ground) welcomed Sunday afternoon strollers. Just before the Bell Shops was the Waldorf Cafeteria, a comfortable haven for sustenance and relaxation while waiting for the train. (Sheldon A. Glew, photographer, FHS Collections.)

In the late 1950s downtown Framingham, just north of the common, reflected the rapid growth in the community. In this image, the local bank has a new digital combination clock/thermometer, all the stores are occupied, and traffic is increasing. Note double headlamps on the newer automobiles. (Sheldon A. Glew, photographer, FHS Collections.)

Islands were drawn on this photograph in the 1950s as part of a traffic study involving the intersection of Hollis and Irving Streets. Only the rotary was built. Forty years later the town is still trying to improve traffic flow at this intersection. (FHS Collections.)

In this 1995 image, traffic whizzes around the traffic island on Concord Street at the junction of Union Avenue and heads toward the railroad crossing. Trains crossing this street have been a source of numerous "studies" for over seventy-five years. The latest proposal is to depress the road under the tracks. Will it happen? (P. Kapteyn, photographer, courtesy *The Middlesex News.*)

Six

Nobscot

Since the earliest settlement of the town, North Framingham has been a busy place. New Boston and Brackett's Corner were early names for the area now known as Nobscot. The Bracketts ran a bakery and store at Nobscot Square for almost one hundred years. The site of Solomon Brackett's Tavern, which stands on the right in this 1904 photograph, is now occupied by an apartment complex and a gas station. The tavern was moved and exists today as a private home. Edmands Road, coming in from the left, was originally an old Native American trail leading to Marlborough. (M.S. Evans, photographer, FHS Collections.)

Called "The Merchant of Nobscot," Elijah Eugene Bacon (1855–1945) was also known as "The Marshall Field of Nobscot." Besides peddling household goods from a horse-drawn wagon and running a store at 82 Edmands Road, E.E. Bacon was a prolific contributor to the Framingham newspaper. (FHS Collections.)

Schoolhouse No. 8 on Edgell Road at Nobscot replaced an older school building in 1854. It was later used by the Grange and the Boy Scouts. In July 1994, fire destroyed the building. The site is now open land under the jurisdiction of the Framingham Conservation Commission. (M.S. Evans, photographer, FHS Collections.)

At the turn of the century the Nobscot Volunteer Fire Department used a "hand tub" to extinguish fires by pumping water from a stream or well onto the fire. (M.S. Evans, photographer, FHS Collections.)

In 1893 a new passenger station at Nobscot opened, replacing an "uncouth affair." The structure was built with the expectation that a spa in the Nobscot Spring area would develop ". . . as the availability and healthfulness of our elevated situations become known." The anticipated mountain hotel was never built. The station still stands near the tracks on Water Street as a private home. (M.S. Evans, photographer, FHS Collections.)

Engine No. 424 is steaming through the village with Nobscot Hill in the background. The track in the foreground is from a siding which extended to Frost Street. The siding was used for freight deliveries and as a passing area for trains. (FHS Collections.)

Healthful water from a natural spring on Edgell Road, near Sudbury, was bottled and shipped as far as New York and Philadelphia. (M.S. Evans, photographer, FHS Collections.)

After the Nobscot Bottling Company closed, people regularly filled their own water bottles from the spring. In the 1980s vandals polluted the area and the town posted a disclaimer. (M.S. Evans, photographer, FHS Collections.)

In 1900 Marcellus Nixon, Warren Nixon's son, posed with his third wife, Addie, in front of the house his father built at 847 Edmands Road. The brick house burned, and later a playhouse was moved to the site. It became the home of Penelope Turton, who ran an organic farm across the street for almost forty years. (M.S. Evans, photographer, FHS Collections.)

Not only was Warren Nixon well known in Framingham history as a surveyor and draftsman, having drawn a map of the town in 1832, he also served as teacher, selectman, justice of the peace, representative to the General Court, and captain in the light infantry company. (FHS Collections.)

102

Revolutionary War Captain Thomas Nixon Jr. (Warren's father) built this house in 1787 at 881 Edmands Road. The house stands today, protected by preservation covenants. Inside, a letter contained in an envelope, on the back of a silhouette which is hanging on a door carved with two hearts, tells the following legend: "A traveler fell in love with the Widow Stone who lived at a hotel at the Centre. He promised to come back and marry her. She, however, married Nixon. A few years later, a man knocked on the door and asked for shelter. Before morning, the former admirer crept downstairs, carved the two hearts on the door, and stole away, while his hosts still slept." (M.S. Evans, photographer, FHS Collections.)

The arched window on the Nixon barn was out for repairs in 1939 when the original barn was destroyed by fire. Another barn was moved to the site and the window installed. Today, the "new" barn, with a road through it, serves as an exit from a small development called Barnbridge. (M.S. Evans, photographer, FHS Collections.)

A farmer gathers in hay from a large field on Water Street at Nobscot. In the middle distance is the Cutting/Eldridge/Bacon house, the aqueduct, a cider mill, a wagon shed, and in the far distance, Nobscot Hill. (FHS Collections.)

Fox hunting at Millwood began in 1866 when Mr. E.F. Bowditch imported some hounds. The Millwood Horse Show started in 1923 and continued through the 1930s at Waveney Farm. Riding sidesaddle required exceptional balance and skill. (C. Holbrook, photographer, FHS Collections.)

A men's dinner of the Millwood Hunt Club was held in George Lampson's barn at Millwood, on Edmands Road, c. 1936, with the horses looking on! The Millwood Hunt ended its 103-year history in 1969. (Hanley, photographer, FHS Collections.)

Located on the shoulder of Gibb's Mountain, Eastleigh Farms featured award-winning Guernsey cows noted for their milk production. This *c.* 1933 photograph shows Mr. Beebe with two of his prized bull calves, Eastleigh Chieftain and Eastleigh David. (Gift of A. Bugley, FHS Collections.)

As the dairy industry in New England fell on hard times, Eastleigh Farms switched to Hereford cattle for beef production. (Gift of A. Bugley, FHS Collections.)

In this *c.* 1898 photograph, Harry Ellsworth Bacon of Nobscot is all decked out in his Spanish-American War uniform. The Musterfield at the intersection of Concord Street and the Worcester Turnpike became a state-wide staging area for troops. (Courtesy the Bacon family, FHS collections.)

Although Framingham had voting privileges for women on the ballot in 1895, it wasn't until 1920 that the 19th Amendment was finally approved by the country. (FHS Collections.)

 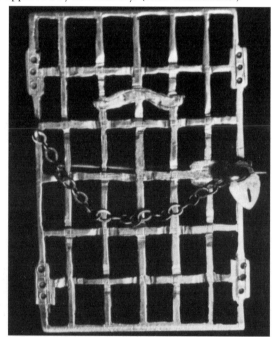

LEFT: Louise Parker Mayo lived on Nixon Road in Nobscot. In 1917, at age forty-six, she went to Washington, D.C., to picket for the right to vote. She was arrested and jailed for four days. (Courtesy Dona Germond.)

RIGHT: After women were finally granted the right to vote, the National Woman's Party awarded silver jail-door pins to about one hundred women who had been jailed for protesting. Louise Mayo's pin was donated to the Framingham Historical Society by her daughter. It has been chosen for reproduction by the Boston Museum of Fine Arts. (John Neister, photographer, FHS Collections.)

This photograph shows a Bacon family reunion, *c.* 1915. From left to right are: (front row) Everett Bacon, Annie Bacon, Grace Foster, Adeline Bacon, and Maggie Finn; (back row) four unidentified men, Ina Cutting, Harry Bacon, Maude Littlefield, William Foster, and Grandma McKeen. (FHS Collections.)

Schoolhouse #7 was built on the corner of Nixon and Edmands Roads in 1839. The building served as a community social hall for a number of years after it was closed as a school. The Society of Friends purchased it in 1964 and moved the building 50 feet back from the road. Today it serves as their meetinghouse. (M.S. Evans, photographer, FHS Collections.)

The name Nobscot comes from the Algonquin word "penobscot," meaning "at the fall of rocks" or "the steep rock place." Early in the seventeenth century eight Nipmuc villages could be seen from the 600-foot summit of Nobscot Hill, which served Native Americans not only as a lookout but also as a place of spiritual significance. Tantamous, a medicine man commonly known as Old Jethro by the colonists, lived on the northwest slope of the mountain with his extended family until the outbreak of King Philip's War in 1675. (George F. Marlowe, photographer, FHS Collections.)

Seven

Route 9

The Worcester Turnpike, a 40-mile stagecoach route for which a toll was charged, opened in 1810. It followed a straight line between Boston and Worcester. The Boston & Worcester trolley operated over the road from 1904 to 1932. Route 9, a "super-highway," was built in the 1930s over the old turnpike road. The Framingham Baseball Club is shown here, about 1880, ready to leave for a game. (S. White, photographer, donated by F.M. Kendall, FHS Collections.)

Samuel, William, Thomas, J. Kittredge, Hollis, Otis, Josiah, and Eliphalet were sons of Thomas and Nabby Abbot Hastings in the middle of the nineteenth century. Thomas and Nabby's ninth son, Dexter, died at age twelve. (FHS Collections.)

Hollis Hastings (1807–1880), one of the nine Hastings brothers, manufactured harnesses and carriages for many years at Framingham Junction, the corner of Old Connecticut Path and Beacon Street, also known as Hastingsville. (*Framingham Illustrated*, 1880.)

Dam No. 3 on the Foss Reservoir at Worcester Road was built as part of a network used to convey water by gravity to metropolitan Boston. Today the city would draw upon the 1.2 billion gallons of water in the Foss only in an emergency; it has not been tapped since the early 1980s. (FHS Collections.)

In this image, Foss Reservoir is at left center and Stearnes Reservoir is at right center, with Route 9 between them. The two reservoirs were part of an eight reservoir complex built in the Sudbury River watershed to provide water for metro Boston. Due to inadequate capacity and concerns about water purity, the complex was taken off line after the completion of the Quabbin Reservoir in the 1930s. (FHS Collections.)

The Musterfield occupied 115 acres south of Route 9 and west of Concord Street on land formerly known as Pratt's Plain. It was the military center of the Commonwealth from 1873 through World War II. Later converted to housing for veterans, the area now contains elderly housing, state Civil Defense Headquarters, and the State Police Academy. (FHS Collections.)

This c. 1887 photograph shows typical military transportation of the day. A member of Battery A, Second Brigade, of the state militia is shown here while the brigade was in camp at the Musterfeld. (FHS Collections.)

Robert Edgar Mayall, Framingham Centre

The Avro

The airplane that has the record of carrying 45,000 passengers WITHOUT A SINGLE ACCIDENT.

This is the machine now being used at the Muster Field by

Brooks, Banks and Smith

Framingham's first airport, housing the U.S. Army Air Service, operated from 1920 to 1923 at the Musterfield. Brooks, Banks, and Smith, listed on the poster above, were pilots. Brooks was a Framingham native who became a World War I ace with six air victories. A restored SPAD XIII biplane, flown by Brooks in the war, is on display at the Smithsonian Air and Space Museum in Washington, D.C. In 1921 the first U.S. air-mail flight to New England flew from Washington, D.C., to Framingham! A truck then took the mail to Boston. Between 1929 and 1946, another airport operated in Framingham on the site where the General Motors plant would later be built. (R.E. Mayall, photographer, FHS Collections.)

Built *c.* 1700 by Caleb Bridges, whose mother was accused of witchcraft and fled to Framingham from Salem, this building served as the clubhouse for the Framingham Country Club from 1902 until the 1950s. Today the building serves as a recreation center for the Edgewater Hills apartments. (FHS Collections.)

Several complexes of six-story apartment buildings were constructed *c.* 1968 on the south side of Route 9, near the Southborough line, triggering a moratorium on buildings of this type which is still in effect today. Meanwhile, the luxury apartments have provided housing for many of Framingham's citizens. Some have been converted to condominiums. (Courtesy Edgewater Apartments.)

The Gates Elm, planted by Jonathan Rugg in 1774, was one of the largest trees in New England, and had a base circumference in excess of 50 feet. You could climb specially constructed stairs onto its limbs, the longest of which extended 120 feet. The root system was damaged when Exit 12 on the Massachusetts Turnpike was constructed, and the tree slowly died. It was felled in 1959. The historic Rugg-Gates house, shown in this picture, still stands on Upper Gates Street. (Courtesy Martha E. Flinter.)

In this photograph four girls are waiting for the trolley on Worcester Road, *c.* 1905. The Centre had a different look prior to the construction of Route 9 in the 1930s and the underpass in 1969. Most of this scene no longer exists. (M.S. Evans, photographer, FHS Collections.)

The old Boston & Worcester trolley-car barn on Worcester Road is today's Trolley Square mall. Containing a frame store, post office, and several other businesses, the building demonstrates the successful re-use of a historic structure. (FHS Collections.)

The Boston & Worcester trolley station at Framingham Junction on Route 9 is pictured here as it appeared in 1908. Concord Street is just out of view on the right. The building also housed the headquarters for the Boston & Worcester Street Railway (trolley) Company. (FHS Collections.)

"They had the best pecan rolls," remembers a former patron of the Abner Wheeler House. The oldest part of the house was built by Joseph Stone around 1722. Owned by Abner Wheeler from 1809 to 1843, the building served as an inn from 1933 until the 1960s. It was torn down in the 1970s to build Deerskin Plaza. (FHS Collections.)

Houston Rawls, developer of Shoppers World, scheduled well-known Swedish actress Anita Eckberg to make a publicity appearance for the mall's opening. Designed by architect Morris Ketchum Jr., Shoppers World was to be "the Main Street of the future." One of the first regional shopping malls, it opened with forty-four shops and services on two levels surrounding a landscaped open-air mall measuring 675 feet by 100 feet. Shoppers World had an enormous impact on post-war commercial architecture. It was demolished in December 1994 to make way for a warehouse-style mall, also called Shoppers World. (Courtesy Framingham Historical Commission, FHS Collections.)

This image of Shoppers World shows the Jordan Marsh anchor store. Its landmark dome was the largest unsupported dome in the country. Designed to look like a flying saucer that had landed, it covered 45,000 square feet of open floor space. (Courtesy Framingham Historical Commission, FHS Collections.)

For more than ten years the north end of Shoppers World remained open, waiting for another anchor store to close the loop. Meanwhile, the gap was used for the kiddie rides shown here and by other temporary exhibits. The north end was finally enclosed in the early 1960s by a Jordan Marsh "basement" store. (Courtesy Framingham Historical Commission, FHS Collections.)

On Shoppers World's opening day in October 1951, "Ask Me" girls provided World Series information to shoppers who didn't want to miss the game. (Peter Besh, photographer, courtesy Framingham Historical Commission, FHS Collections.)

"Congratulations! You just won the TV set!" A promotion held in 1964 was designed to attract more customers to Shoppers World. (Courtesy Framingham Historical Commission, FHS Collections.)

A typical American family strolls through Shoppers World in 1951. The original press release for Shoppers World called it a "Homemaker's Dream." Gas was cheap and abundant, and mothers were ready to get out of the house. Shoppers World was a destination point for America's love affair with the automobile after World War II. (Peter Besh, photographer, FHS Collection.)

In this photograph, a family enjoys an outdoor summer concert in the courtyard of Shoppers World in 1962. Concerts were held every summer until the mall closed in 1994. Note the cinema marquee. (Courtesy Framingham Historical Commission, FHS Collections.)

The Sculos family's restaurant, pictured *c.* 1940, was named "Maridor" for daughters Mary and Dora. Its success led to the addition of the Fonda Del Corro motel in 1961. In 1983, under a new owner, the restaurant became "Duca's at the Maridor." The site, located at Route 9 and Prospect Street, is now a shopping center. (FHS Collections.)

A favorite 1940s nightspot on Route 9, the Meadows was built by singer Vaughn Monroe, who broadcast his "Camel Caravan" radio program from here starting in 1946. The building became "Beefsteak Charlie's" between 1972 and 1979. It burned in December 1980. Bennigan's and The Meadows office building are now on the site. (FHS Collections.)

"For the very best in Steaks and Seafood" advertised the Sea 'N Surf, located on Route 9 westbound, 1/3 mile beyond Shoppers World. You could pick your own lobster from their pool. (Courtesy of Elaine Fader.)

Near the Southborough line, on the westbound side of Route 9, is a site long associated with restaurants. Originally the location of Josiah Temple's (1815–93) home, the spot has been successively occupied by the Viking Restaurant, Eddie Curran's, Christy's, the Red Coach Grill, El Torrito, and now Chef Orient. Old-timers remember musicians "jamming" at Christy's following local gigs. (FHS Collections.)

The Spa at Echo Springs, located west of today's Edgewater Hills apartments near Exit 12 of the Mass Pike, offered sandwiches and ice cream from the Echo Farm Dairy. (FHS Collections.)

Barometric Spring was known to Native Americans and is described in Temple's *History of Framingham* (1887). Its flow varied with the barometric pressure. The site was disrupted when the Massachusetts Turnpike was built. Water cascading down the rock cut of Exit 12 is the most visible reminder of this former landmark. (FHS collections.)

Dr. Amar G. Bose, professor of electrical engineering at MIT, founded Bose Corporation in 1964. In addition to producing superior sound systems that are installed in major venues around the world and in fine automobiles, the company manufactures a variety of home audio products. Bose Corporation today employs over 4,000 people worldwide; 1,200 employees are located in Framingham facilities. (Bose is a registered trademark. Courtesy of the Bose Corporation.)

Known from early times as "The Mountain," the prominent land formation at center right rose 160 feet above the surrounding terrain and was about 3/8 of a mile in diameter. In 1958, over one million cubic yards of soil were removed and used in building the Massachusetts Turnpike. BOSE is completing a building at the top of the industrial park on the Mountain. (Courtesy of the Bose Corporation.)

The new Route 9 super-highway, *c.* early 1930s, was lined with trees and residences. This photograph was taken near the cloverleaf intersection with Concord Street. The cars in the right lane are heading east. (Courtesy South Middlesex Area Chamber of Commerce, FHS Collections.)

Today Route 9 at the Framingham/Natick line is called "The Golden Mile" because of its high concentration of retail and service establishments. Heavily congested traffic, especially at rush hours, lumbers east and west over one of the state's most heavily traveled roads—and it all began with the stagecoach. (*Framingham 275th Anniversary*, courtesy Town of Framingham.)